To Nell
from

Apples of Gold

APPLES OF GOLD

New and Inspiring Messages of

PETER MARSHALL

Selected by Stanley Hendricks

Illustrated by Richard Hook

♔ HALLMARK EDITIONS

CONTENTS

'A MAN CALLED PETER'

The name of Peter Marshall is familiar today to millions of Americans who know his inspiring life story as "a man called Peter" in Catherine Marshall's best-selling biography of that title. Peter Marshall came to the United States from Scotland as a young man with a profound belief that his life would be dedicated to the service of Christ. Despite difficulties that at times seemed insurmountable, he was ordained to the ministry of the Presbyterian Church.

In her book, Catherine Marshall describes her husband, the man whom God made "real to those who listened":

"Peter Marshall was a tall, well-built young man with the broad shoulders of a football player, camouflaged by his Geneva gown. His hair, which had been very blond, was turning darker. It was curly, never slicked down, inclined to be a little unruly.

"His face was handsome in a rugged sort of way. There was in it a combination of gentleness and humor along with forcefulness and strength.

"He seemed thoroughly at home in a pulpit. While he preached, he frequently used gestures, but they

were never strained or artificial. Most of his empha-
sis was made with his voice—an extraordinarily res-
onant speaking voice, flexible, dramatic, with a clear,
precise diction.

"But more than these superficialities was the in-
disputable fact that, under the impact of this man's
praying and preaching, God became real to those
who listened. While Peter led them in worship, God
was no longer a remote, theological abstraction, but
a loving Father, who was interested in each individual, who stooped to man's smallest need. So men
and women, who were hungry for the love of God,
came back again and again."

From an eventful pastorate in Atlanta, Georgia,
Peter Marshall was called to lead the congregation
of the historic New York Avenue Presbyterian
Church in Washington, D.C., where he served during the late 1930's and throughout World War II. In
1947 Dr. Marshall was appointed Chaplain to the
United States Senate. It was his duty to deliver the
daily prayers at the beginning of each Senate ses-
sion. He infused new life and spirit into them and
they began to draw national attention.

Peter Marshall died of a heart attack on January
25, 1949. Among the legacies of love he left behind
were more than 600 sermons written in his distinc-
tive style. *Apples of Gold* offers four of those messages which have never before been published.

The Words of PETER MARSHALL

APPLES OF GOLD

A word fitly spoken
is like apples of gold
in pictures of silver.

PROVERBS 25:11

It is a dangerous matter for the preacher to take a text in the Book of Wisdom. Yet this particular text is an intriguing one.

One wonders just what the metaphor means—"apples of gold" could be several things.

There are those who believe the reference is to the apricot, gleaming golden amid the bright yet pale foliage.

Others incline to the view that the writer had in mind fruit carved in gold and set in dainty work of silver—as brilliant a piece of decoration as can well be imagined.

But whatever the metaphor means, one thing is clear: a "word fitly spoken" is a lovely thing. This finely turned metaphor gives to it the highest possible praise.

Words are freighted nowadays with life or death, with simple truth or sinister falsehood. On every wavelength, words are whispered or shouted around the world in a propaganda war in which the guns are ideas
   and the bullets are words.
Words are like arrows shot into the air that come to

earth we know not where. Sometimes they find lodg-
ment in the hearts of those whom we love—and
whom we would not deliberately stab with daggers
   yet wound with careless speech.

They are like feathers blown by the wind: once scat-
tered, they can never be reclaimed.

We can all think of words that we ought not to have
spoken
   words that we would give anything to recall.

We even say, in shame and penitence:
   "I take back what I said"
but we can never really take it back.

No more can the plucked flower be joined again to
its stem
   or the cracked egg-shell be made whole
No more can the snowflake that melts in the river
find its first shape again, than can we bring back the
foolish, impetuous word that went out to sting
   to hurt
      or to offend.
The damage done, we can pluck out the thorn
   but the pain of it lingers.

If we did not already know it in our own hearts and

in our lives, James warns us in his epistle:

"The tongue is a fire, world of iniquity . . .
the tongue can no man tame;
it is an unruly evil, full of deadly poison.
Therewith bless we God, even the Father;
and therewith curse we men, which are made after
the likeness of God.
Out of the same mouth proceedeth blessing and
cursing. . . ."

Yes, James, we know. The solemn thing about words
is that before you speak them, you are their master.
After you speak them, they are your master.

It is a solemn thought that sometime, somewhere, we
shall be judged according to our words. For Christ
has told us:

"Every idle word that men shall speak, they shall
give account thereof in the day of judgment. For
by thy words thou shalt be justified, and by thy
words thou shalt be condemned."

But right now let us think particularly of the words
spoken fitly—the words which are like apples of
gold.

Perhaps the classic example in modern times is the
reference in the speech of Winston Churchill to the
heroic work of the R.A.F. during the Battle of Britain,

when the German air force hurled its might against England. Said the Prime Minister;

"The gratitude of every home in our Island,
in our Empire,
   and indeed throughout the whole world
goes out to the British airmen, who,
   undaunted by odds
      unwearied in their constant challenge
and mortal danger,
are turning the tide of the World War by their
prowess and by their devotion.

Never in the field of human conflict was so much owed by so many to so few."

One suspects that in the speeches of Churchill will be found many a word fitly spoken, for he is a master of words.

So too was Lincoln. The more I think about the Gettysburg Address, the more I am convinced that his words that day were fitly spoken, and what he said then could not be said in a better way.

Who could improve upon his:
"We cannot dedicate
   we cannot consecrate
      we cannot hallow this ground.

The brave men, living and dead, who struggled
here, have consecrated it far above our poor power
to add or detract.

The world will little note, nor long remember,
what we say here; but it can never forget what
they did here. . . .That this nation, under God,
shall have a new birth of freedom, and that gov-
ernment of the people,

by the people
and for the people
shall not perish from the earth.''

On the walls of a college of Oxford University hangs
a letter of Lincoln's as a model of purest English,
rarely, if ever, surpassed. It is his letter to Mrs. Bixby
of Boston.

"Dear Madam,

I have been shown in the files of the War De-
partment a statement of the Adjutant General of
Massachusetts that you are the mother of five
sons who have died gloriously on the field of
battle.

I feel how weak and fruitless must be any word
of mine which should attempt to beguile you from
the grief of a loss so overwhelming.

But I cannot refrain from tendering you the
consolation that may be found in the thanks of the
republic they died to save. I pray that our Heav-

enly Father may assuage the anguish of your be-
reavement, and leave you only the cherished
memory of the loved and lost, and the solemn
pride that must be yours to have laid so costly a
sacrifice upon the altar of freedom.

    Yours very sincerely and respectfully,
      A. Lincoln.''

There are words of warning and advice that are fitly
spoken, and many a successful man can look back to
the day when somebody warned him, or gave him
good advice that proved to be a turning point in his
life.
Or perhaps it was a word of encouragement or praise
that helped someone to keep on
    to persevere
and in the end to succeed.

Such words are all too rare.

There is a lovely story about George Washington
when he took command of the Continental Army at
Cambridge, Massachusetts. He found a ragged body
of soldiers. Some of them had uniforms, some had
none.
  Some had guns
    some had sticks
      others had only the implements which they

had brought from their farms.

A regiment from Connecticut looked particularly untidy. The men were few

badly armed

and poorly dressed.

They did not even stand at attention. Their ranks were ragged and they had the air of discouragement. Many of them were hungry and had gone without a decent meal for days on end.

Some were lame. They were a sorry lot.

Yet when the regiment was drawn up for Washington to inspect them, the great General stood erect and, looking at them as if they were in the finest regiment in the world, he said:

"Gentlemen, I have great confidence in the
men of Connecticut."

One of the soldiers writing home to his family said in his letter,

"When I heard Washington say that, I clasped my
musket to my breast and said to myself,

'Let them come on.'"

A word of encouragement means more than we can possibly imagine. Think how many people there are in this world who are hungry to hear someone say a word of encouragement

a word of cheer

to keep up morale

to give courage.

Although we often say things on the impulse that we ought not to say, there is never anything wrong with words of encouragement to those who are doing good work.

And what shall we say about the words of testimony which have the power to strengthen and make brave others whose faith is made strong and vital by the contagion of another's witness?

There is many a young man or a young woman in America who will be a better Christian because of what you said about the church and about Christ
about things worthwhile
about prayer
and the constant fight to keep the pennants
of one's allegiance from dragging in the mud.

On one of the first visits to this country of the great Japanese Christian Toyohiko Kagawa, he attended a student conference on the West Coast. One of the student delegates burst out rather impatiently:
"We are wasting our time discussing Christianity. Christianity has failed."
Kagawa quietly replied: "Mine hasn't."

There was a word fitly spoken, a word of testimony with the power to convince.

Carl Wallace Petty in his devotional book *Evening Altar* tells of a visit he made to an old lady whose life had been lived in unselfish devotion and hard work.

She had lived for others, in service late and early, and now as her life was running out, she lay in her last sickness. Dr. Petty tells how he tried to comfort her—but she was worried.

One thing troubled her, and that was what she would say to the Lord when she saw Him, because she had never been able to express herself; she would not know what to say or how to say it.

Her pastor said: "Why, you won't have to say a thing. Just show Him your hands."

When we turn to the New Testament we find from the lips of Jesus Christ so many words fitly spoken that we are embarrassed to choose among them.

For my own part I shall always regard what the Lord said to Jairus as apples of gold in pictures of silver.

You remember the occasion?

Jairus, a ruler of the synagogue, had come to beg Jesus to return with him to heal his little daughter— a girl of twelve, who was dangerously ill.

In response to the urgent call of the father, Jesus

turned and was on His way when, passing through the crowded streets, a certain woman touched the hem of His garment and was healed of her twelve-year-long malady. Everyone knows that lovely story. In the excitement of that healing, news came from the home of Jairus that his little girl had died, and concluded the messengers with the finality of human despair,

"Why trouble the Master any further? It is
all over. It is too late."

Hearing their sorrowful conclusion, Jesus said to the stricken father:

"Have no fear, only believe."

There are apples of gold—words fitly spoken as only the Lord can speak them

words of comfort to bereaved hearts
words that bring hope and peace.

Perhaps there are hearts here in this place that need to hear such words:

"Have no fear, only believe."

There is a picture that shines with the softest colors of the mercy of God.

GOOD MEDICINE

A merry heart doeth good like a medicine.

PROVERBS 17:22

I believe that for summer days, a sermon should be light, with a lift to it,

> cheerful,
> practical,
> and short.

Therefore I have chosen for my text a verse from the Book of Proverbs.

In the Authorized Version, it reads:

> "A merry heart doeth good like a medicine."

Moffatt translates it:

> "A glad heart helps and heals."

The American Revised Version translates it:

> "A cheerful heart is a good medicine."

Well, there you have the idea:

> "A glad heart,
> a merry heart,
> a cheerful heart is good medicine."

I am sure you will agree.

When you greet a friend with the question: "Well, how are you today?" you would not expect your friend to say: "Oh, I don't feel very good. You see, I have a sore back, and I'm not sleeping well these days. Then, too, I think my blood pressure is getting a bit high. You know, I have a vitamin deficiency, and if you are interested, I'd like to tell you the funniest thing about my operation two years ago. . . ."

At that point, you would probably remember an appointment to make, and try to get away as quickly as possible.

On the other hand, what a joy it is to greet a friend who in answer to your query: "How are you this morning?" says, with a shining face,

"Oh I'm fine! I'm all right."

Why, it makes you feel better just to hear the optimism in his voice and to see the joy in his face. Such people are an inspiration.

You may have heard the story that is told about John Quincy Adams, who lived to be over eighty. In his later years, a friend met him on the street in Boston, and greeted him: "How is John Quincy Adams this morning?"

The old man replied:

"John Quincy Adams is very well, I thank you. The house he is living in is getting old and ramshackled, and one of these days he is going to have to move out; but as far as John Quincy Adams himself is concerned, he is very well, I thank you."

"A cheerful heart is a good medicine." Yes. But the verse in Proverbs adds a contrasting thought:
  "But a broken spirit drieth up the bones."
Or as Moffatt puts it,
      "saps vitality."

"A broken spirit saps vitality." Isn't it so!
When our feelings are hurt, when our hearts are wounded, when our spirits are low, our vitality also is lowered. We say we have no "pep." The heart is taken out of us, we say—we have little enthusiasm. When our feelings are hurt, and we are wounded in spirit, it may well be more serious than any physical injury.

You know, there are different kinds of Christians. There are Martha Christians, who are so busy in the kitchen getting lunch ready for the others that they miss all the programs, the interesting talks, and so on—
Or like that noble company of our Sunday School staff, who give all of Sunday morning looking after the children so that their parents can go to church, so that they never get the chance to join the rest of us in worship.

They never hear the music or the sermon, because they are Martha Christians. Thank God for them.

Then there are the Mary Christians, who want to meditate and enjoy the spiritual inspirations of the music and the worship and the sermons and the instructions, and never think of the more practical aspects of church work.

They are the people who come to church regularly, and *get* all the time—and never think of *giving*.

Then there are the grandstand Christians, who are quite willing to say nice things about their fellow Christians who are doing the work, as long as they themselves can sit in the stands and enjoy the results of other people's labors.

There are also cemetery Christians—those who are always turning back to old sorrows
    keeping the flowers fresh on old graves
        nursing old wounds and keeping them from
        healing by opening them up on every occasion
    re-hashing past mistakes and wrongs and keeping
    alive ghosts of the past that would fain lie
    down and die, if they were permitted to do so.
In Christ, it is our privilege to forget, and it is our duty to forgive.

Some people think that the saints were sad, solemn souls, and that if you are very good, you must be very serious.

It is not so.

The saints were merry men, who went singing through the world incredibly happy, for they had a certain secret in their hearts.

One evening, St. Francis of Assisi sat in the light of the setting sun, and a little boy nestled by his side with a chessboard, and they began to play a game together.

An austere Brother came upon them, and said:

"For shame, Brother Francis, that you should play a foolish game with a foolish child. [By the way, nobody who knows anything about chess would ever call it foolish.] If the Lord were suddenly to appear, what would you do?"

"What would I do?" asked Francis, with a radiant smile and a twinkle in his eye.
"Brother, it is a foolish question.
I would finish the game.
It was for the glory of God that I began it."

On another day, the news had gone round that Francis was to spend the night in a little town. The town turned out to do him honor, and the chief official had an address to read to the visitor. When Francis, approaching, saw the display, his heart sank. Then, at the entrance of the town, he saw some children playing on a seesaw.

He joined them, and began to go up and down on the seesaw. Now it is difficult to read a solemn address to a man bobbing up and down on a seesaw. So the official pocketed his address, and the people went away saying that he was not a saint, but a clown. Francis, chuckling to himself, went to his modest lodgings, glad to be free of the solemn, silly ceremony.

Why were the saints so happy?
The answer is easy.
They had no selfishness
    and they had no fear.
        They sought nothing for themselves
            and they were afraid of nothing.

If we observe a really happy man, we do not find him thinking about happiness, much less talking about it. He is either building a boat,

                writing a poem,
                growing roses,

        puttering in his basement,
       fighting for some great cause,
     playing with his grandchildren,
  or hunting for dinosaur eggs in the Gobi desert.
He 's not talking.

Happiness is not necessary to existence. A man once told Emerson that the world was coming to an end next week.

    "Never mind;" said Emerson, "we can get along
    without it."

Some people seem to be able to get along without happiness.

Maybe Abraham Lincoln was not a very happy man, at least in his years as President.
They say that Mark Twain, who made millions of other people happy, was seldom happy himself.

There is the well-known fact that some of the most successful clowns were men with broken hearts.

Some people have to get along without happiness.
  They were not made for it.
    They do not know how to be happy.
      They would not know what to do with happi-
       ness were it to come to them.

Yet Jesus said:

> "I am come that ye might have life, and have
> it abundantly. . . . I am come that your joy
> might be full."

But how can we have cheerful hearts?

First of all, we must rid our hearts of all that is
wrong and sinful. For it is apparent, as we have
found out, that we cannot do wrong and feel right.
We have to rid ourselves of the feelings of guilt for
what we have done wrong. And the only way this
can be done is through confession to God and accept-
ance of the forgiveness of Him Who said:

> "Though thy sins be as scarlet, they shall be as
> white as snow; though they be red like crimson,
> they shall be as wool."

When we have repented of sins and wrongs, and
have confessed them, we may be assured of God's
pardon, and that God has put them behind His back,
and will remember them against us no more.

Let us then put them behind our backs too, and let
them stay buried.

When Martin Luther was facing great difficulties
and great dangers as the Reformation movement

spread, he was often discouraged and depressed.

During one of his periods of despondency, his wife appeared at breakfast one morning, dressed in deep mourning. When he asked her why, she solemnly replied: "God is dead." Then she added,

> "Unless God is dead, I do not see how you could possibly be so discouraged and dejected."

Sometimes we act as if God were dead
      had vacated His throne
   had abdicated.

Not so. God is still upon the throne. The Kingdom of our Lord will come upon the earth and His Will yet shall be done.

Paul was persuaded that "all things work together for good to them that love God." I believe that is still true.

You remember on the last night before His crucifixion, Jesus gathered His disciples in that upper room and spoke to them of the things that shortly were to happen.

Their hearts were filled with foreboding. The atmosphere was heavy with nameless dreads, and they were apprehensive.

It was then He said to them:
"Let not your heart be troubled.
Believe in God. Believe also
in Me."
Then a little later He said:
"In this world ye shall have
tribulation, but cheer up! I
have overcome the world."
"Cheer up," says Jesus.
"Cheer up!" "I have overcome the world". . . . "and My grace is sufficient for you". . . ."have no fear, only believe". . . ."Lo, I am with you always, even unto the end of the world."

His grace is all that we need. . . .
prayer is our secret weapon. . . .
His presence with us our adequate protection. . . .
His Spirit our shield and guide. . . .
and our faith the guarantee of our ultimate victory.

"This is the victory that overcometh the world, even our faith."

THE HANDS OF GOD

. . . Behold my hands.

JOHN 20:27

You will recall that on the first occasion when the Risen Christ appeared to His disciples, when He first took form among them, although the door did not open . . . there was one of their number who was not present.

Thomas was not with them, and the record does not tell us where he was.

I have imagined him alone nursing his grief, his disappointment, alone, perhaps in the garden on the Mount of Olives that overlooked the Holy City.

Perhaps seated on a rock, his chin cupped in his hands, and his dazed, tear-filled eyes watching the twinkling lights of the Holy City . . . .
feeling the pain of his broken heart
and the crashing of his hopes.

When Thomas returned to join the group, he heard the announcement told breathlessly
with shining eyes
as they gripped him by the arm
that the Master had appeared unto them, and that they knew—beyond any doubt—that He was alive. Partly because of his overwhelming grief, and partly because he was by nature and disposition a skeptic, Thomas would not believe them.

He was, as it were, from some Palestinean Missouri
   he had to be shown
      he demanded proof
         he insisted that he would not be swept
            off his feet by any emotional reaction
he would have to be sure
               and he refused to believe until the Lord
               should appear before him
and until he could stick his unbelieving finger into
the nailprints of the hands of the Son of God.

Before very long the disciples were again united in
the room, and the door still being closed, and without bothering to knock, Jesus stood before them.

He held out His hands to Thomas and said to that
disciple with the great, big wondering eyes:
   "Thomas, behold My hands."

It was enough for Thomas, and it drew him to his
glorious surrender: "My Lord, and my God!"

In the hope that a look at the hands of the Master
might bring to you the same assurance, I invite you
now to examine the hands of Christ.

Architecturally, the hand is a marvelous instrument.
It can be expressive, and gestures with the hand can

be more eloquent than many words.

There are those who claim that hidden in the palm of the hand lie the destinies and the fortune—good or bad—of life itself.

While there may be some connection between the markings in the palm of your hand and your nature or characteristics, I do not believe that anyone is able by studying the lines in your hand to tell you anything about the future, or anything about yourself that you did not already know.

There are all kinds of hands.

There are the pale hands of the song, like lotus buds, soft and white and coldly beautiful.

But as far as I am concerned, there is a greater beauty in my mother's hands as I remember them
    they were warm and soft and red
      some of the finger-tips were rough with
        household care
And there are the hands of the surgeon—strong
        skillful
    deft—yet tender
the hands of the artist
    the hands of the musician—fingers long and

tapering, holding a wondrous skill. . .

There are the hands of the farmer and the laborer—
strong and rough—yet holding a kindness that beauty
never knew.

The hand, however wonderful and intricate its
construction, can be used in many ways.

There is the hand of scorn
    the pointing finger of accusation
        the clenched fist
    the hand upraised to strike
        the begging hand
    the hand of benediction
        the hand of the thief
            the hand clasped in prayer.

The loveliest hands of all are the hands of Jesus of
Nazareth.

They were human hands—the hands of a man—
These are the only hands we can truly appreciate.

After His resurrection, Jesus said
    "Touch me, see I am not a spirit.
    Doth a spirit have flesh and bones as ye see Me
    have?"

You will remember that the two disciples who set out to walk from Jerusalem to Emmaus, and with whom Jesus went as their unknown companion, when He reached out, took bread in His hands and broke it. . .

When they saw His hands, they knew it was Jesus
  they recognized His hands
    they saw the marks of the nails
    the marks of crucifixion that cannot be
    duplicated
or they recognized the gesture.

They saw His hands and knew Him right away. They were hands they were familiar with, hands like their own, save for the scars of the nails.

There were some in later years who tried to deny that Jesus was really a man, but none of the disciples would ever have fallen for that. They saw that He was flesh of our flesh

    like as we are
  and yet without sin.

They knew and we know that you cannot nail a phantom to a tree. They knew and we know that a ghost cannot drive money-changers out of the temple with a whip of rope.

They knew and we know that a specter cannot gather
children in his arms,
    that an optical illusion cannot sit at the
    table and eat with his friends
    that a hypnotic vision cannot say "behold My
    hands"

that a spirit cannot be raised up on a cross—
no, indeed.

This is the first bond that brings us close to Him—
when we know that He walked the earthly trail
before us
    that there is no pain or circumstance He has
    not tasted
        no ache He has not known
            no sorrow that was not also His sorrow
                no joy to which He is a stranger.

He loved the flowers
    He enjoyed the singing of the birds
        He admired sunsets and good music
He loved the out-of-doors—the trees
        the hills
    and the rocks.
He thrilled to a storm, the lancing and the stabbing
of lightning in the hills, the deep rumbling of
the thunder among the mountains.

He enjoyed the sea breeze and the wind in His hair...

The fragrance of the orange groves and the pomegranate delighted His nostrils...

He knew what it was to be tired and to enjoy the delicious gift of sleep.

They saw tears running down His cheeks and smiles tug at the corners of His mouth.

Jesus had a human hand—four fingers and a thumb —a carpenter's hand, it was, one that had gripped the plane and the saw, that had wielded the hammer and held the nail.

Yes, they were human hands—just like ours—
    hands that were sensitive to heat and cold
        hands that could bleed as well as bless.

When Christ walked out of the grave, to resurrection,
    it was in the same body
        He walked on the same wounded feet
            and that earthly body was given adjustment
            to the needs of a spiritual and eternal
            realm.

But that body—

these human hands He extended to Thomas—was the germ or seed of the incorruptible glory in which He now lives.

Here is our infinite comfort and strength—

"Behold My hands," says Jesus. That gives us confidence, and by this we know that the hands that today lay bricks
> dig ditches
> plant flowers
> operate street cars
> mine coal
> wield shovels
> hold riveting machines
> use typewriters
> wrap packages
> wash dishes

shall some day be occupied with the affairs of God in the New Jerusalem.

These are the hands that shall bring the trophies to the feet of the King.

Look again at the hands of the Master—they are human hands.

His hands were also divine, for they have power in

them that never man knew
and with them He touched blind eyes and opened
them to the glory of the sunset
 with them He touched diseased flesh and made
 it clean
  with them He thrilled new life into
  paralyzed limbs
   with them He liberated the cripple
   from his crutch.

We find it mysterious that in a mortal body God
could dwell—all the fullness of the God-head bodily
—that to us is a mystery—a mystery that deepens as
we think of these hands spread out on a beam of
wood, and fastened down with nails.

We are amazed that impious hands could touch His,
that cruel, insensitive fingers could hold Him by the
arm. . .

We wonder that they were not stricken dead
 we wonder that a shock of divine power did
 not paralyze their black hearts
  the wonder is that they survived.

Yes, His hands are divine, for they shaped the
worlds in their infancy—they fashioned the snowflake—"Ensculpted and embossed with His gravers

of wind and His hammers of frost."

He scooped out the earth's basins of clay and filled them with the seven seas. His are the hands that notched the fern and moulded the leaf
    that painted the butterfly's wing
        crimsoned the petal
            laid down the green carpet
                and hung the mighty lanterns in
                the sky.

These are truly the hands of the Master.

He did not come to be an artist—and yet He has painted pictures—if you have eyes to see.

He did not come as a musician, yet He has set a new song in the hearts of men—if you have ears to hear.

He did not come as an author, yet He has written books. You will find them in the Bible, and the stories of His coming, and the tales of His going among men can be read in regenerated lives.

Ah, yes, He had power in His hands, for they are the very same hands that inscribed the tablets of stone with the Law of God
    that wrote on the wall at Belshazzar's feast

       the hands that stopped the lions' mouths
           the hands that healed the lepers
       cured the blind
     the hands that are writing now in your soul
the judgment and spelling out peace.

And they were clean hands. Not in the physical
sense—for they had to be washed. The Carpenter's
hands were not always clean, nor were they always
soft, but they were clean in the sense that His hands
were pure, that in His heart there was no sin.

His hands were not soiled with cruelty
        or with ambition
    or selfishness
but were clean as only innocence can make them.
This is the testimony of all who knew Him—
His friends and enemies alike.

The one who betrayed Him with a kiss said:
   "I have betrayed innocent blood."

The one who as a judge reviewed His case and was
himself forever judged, said of Him,
    "I find no fault in this man."

The captain of the soldiers when the job of crucifixion
was done, said with a new note in his voice:

"This was a righteous man."

"Behold His hands"—this one of whom friend and foe alike bore testimony.

Behold His hands! If you can find any spot upon them, the world will listen to you. Men for ages have tried to find a fault in Him. He has for 20 centuries been under the microscope of criticism. . . .

And yet He still stands with His hands extended where men can examine them, so that they will say with Sidney Lanier:
  "Thou Paragon of Virtue
  Thou Crystal Christ."

They are kind hands
  tender, sympathetic
      the hands of a Friend Who went about doing
      good and Who carries on His work today.

They are hands that are ready to comfort, ready to bless, and all the warmer since now they are wounded hands.

Thomas saw them. We see them. The wounds in His hands are like open mouths to tell us of the love of God.

No longer can men say God does not care when they look at the hands of Jesus.

No longer can men say God does not love when they look at the cross.

When Jesus held out His hands to Thomas, it was for a purpose—in order that Thomas might believe—and you will remember that He said to Thomas:
"Because thou hast seen, thou hast believed,
but blessed are they that have not seen
and yet have believed."

There was the last beatitude—the last blessedness for you and me—and for all who though they did not see Him in the flesh
though they did not see the sunlight on
His hair
though they did not with their eyes see
the wounds in His palms
yet believed that the wounded hands were the hands of God.

As the hands were held out to Thomas, so are they held out to you. He has been holding them out for a long time in invitation.
"Come unto me all ye that labor and are
heavy laden, and I will give you rest."

"Whosoever will may come."

"Him that cometh unto me, I shall in no wise cast out."

What more can God do?

"All day long have I stretched forth my hand." What more can God do, if you will not come?

A BABY'S CRY

And when she had opened it, she saw the
child; and behold, the babe wept.
And she had compassion on him, and said,
This is one of the Hebrews' children.

EXODUS 2:6

The story of Moses, the baby floating in a basket among the bulrushes, is familiar to every child in Sunday School, and will be remembered, however vaguely, by adults long out of Sunday School.

The Israelites were in bondage in Egypt. They were slaves, and their forced labor made life easy and comfortable for the Egyptians. But Pharaoh became alarmed by the way in which the Hebrews were gaining power and strength. Their numbers were increasing, and eventually their majority would be a threat to this easy life.

So Pharaoh issued an order that all male children of the Israelites should be thrown into the river. There would be no more boy babies to grow up to strong manhood, no danger of a brave young boy growing up to be a liberator.

Well, Pharaoh can issue his decree, but it cannot touch the one whom God has chosen to set His people free.

You cannot cancel God's purposes by issuing mandates against them.

The decree of Pharaoh cannot touch Moses.
    Goliath's laughter cannot frighten David, nor

his armor withstand the shepherd lad who is
on the side of the Lord.

The flames of the furnace cannot consume
the Hebrew children
Herod's soldiers, their swords blunted with
slaughter, cannot touch the Babe in the manger
the storm cannot capsize the boat in which
rides the Pilot of Galilee.

When Jesus was buried in the tomb, they sealed the grave, setting upon it the official seals of Rome.

Pilate gave orders to make the grave as secure as they could. They mounted soldiers and took every precaution. But they could not keep Jesus in the tomb.

The seals of empire cannot stop the working out of God's purposes in the world. Not all the soldiers of the legion can halt the God of the Universe.

All the unbelief in the world does not make the Bible untrue. All the devils in and out of Hell cannot destroy the soul whose trust is in the Lord. Hang on to that truth. You will need it someday, in some dark hour when troubles come upon you.

Under the shadow of Pharaoh's edict, a male child was born in the house of Levi. He was a fine baby and his mother, loving him, protected him for three months from the death to which he was born. We are not told what they named this baby. Maybe he did not have a name.

His mother kept him hidden and bending over his secret cradle, watching it by day and by night, she nursed her child until he could no longer be hidden.

Then she made a cradle that would float on the water, and in it she placed her child, and left him hidden among the tall rushes by the river's bank, posting the baby's sister nearby, so that she could keep her eye on developments and know what happened.

When Billy Sunday told this story, he said:
"Some people wonder what angels do. Why, God had a couple of angels on special patrol that day; one to keep the crocodiles away from the baby, and the other to pinch the baby and make him cry at the right time."

At any rate, the crocodiles stayed away, and the baby did cry.

The daughter of Pharaoh, coming down the river for her daily bath, spied the floating cradle and sent a maid to recover it.

The pinching angel was right at hand, for we read that when Pharaoh's daughter peered into the cradle and opened up the blankets, "behold, the babe wept."

Now there is nothing strange or unusual about a baby crying. But the baby had not been crying as the cradle floated, rocking slightly and half hidden at the water's edge.

The tears of the baby did not come until they could melt the heart of the Egyptian princess. Watching from her nearby vantage point, the baby's sister came forward at that juncture and offered to find a nurse for the baby.

This appealed to the daughter of Pharaoh, and she consented. So off went the girl and brought her own mother, the baby's mother, and she thus became, by order of Pharaoh's daughter, the official nurse to her own child:

> "Take the child and nurse it, and I will give thee thy wages."

The baby grew and was brought up as the adopted son of this Egyptian princess. She gave him a name, Moses, because, she said, I drew him out of the water.

That was his name—his only name—and it was to become a famous name. That boy, who grew to be a man, became a famous man, recognized as one of the greatest lawgivers, scholars, and leaders the world has ever known. Isn't it strange to reflect that all this happened because of the most natural thing you can think of—the baby cried at just the right moment!

If we knew everything, we would be amazed what tiny and apparently insignificant events are the hinges for great things to turn on.

Some sixty years ago a father, mother and their young son journeyed from England into Scotland for a summer vacation. The boy one day found an inviting swimming hole, and like any other boy, took off his clothes and jumped in.

Seized with cramps, he shouted for help.

It happened that in a nearby field a farm boy was working, and hearing the cries for help, came running, and diving in, dragged the young English boy out of the water.

The father was very grateful and the next day he called at the farmer's cottage to meet the youth who had saved his son's life.

"What do you plan to do with your life?" he asked.

"Oh, I suppose I'll be a farmer like my father," the boy answered.

"Is there something else you would rather do?"

"Oh, yes, I have always wanted to be a doctor," answered the Scottish boy. "But we are poor people, and we could never afford to pay for my education."

"Never mind that," said the English gentleman. "You shall have your heart's desire and study medicine. Make your plans and I will take care of the costs."
So the boy became a doctor.

In December 1943, Winston Churchill was dangerously ill with pneumonia somewhere in North Africa. His doctor asked Sir Alexander Fleming, the discoverer of the new wonder drug penicillin, to fly over to Africa to attend the sick statesman. Taking off in a fast bomber, Sir Alexander Fleming arrived within a few hours, administered the drug, and for the second time in Churchill's career, saved his life—for it was the boy Winston Churchill whom he had pulled out of the swimming hole so many years before.

"Behold, the babe wept."

The baby cried. God could have performed a miracle here had He so desired. But the baby was just an ordinary baby, doing an ordinary thing, crying. Nothing astounding in that, but it accomplished the purpose.

The princess had pity on the crying infant, for nothing stirs our pity like a baby's tears.

Thus God used a natural means for a great victory.

That is the thing we so often forget—namely that God usually works out His program by the natural means of time and things.

We often expect God to send chariots from Heaven
    to write messages in the sky
      to set aside natural laws and suspend
    the operation of the very principles
    upon whose trustworthiness we depend.
God often works things out by natural means.

We cry for mountains to be moved and they remain fixed where the earth has heaved them up. We beg that the loaves and the fishes might again for our sakes be multiplied. He does not seem to do it.

We pray that we might be saved from the inevitable

consequences of our own stupidity, but He refuses to suspend laws for our benefit.

Yet the day of miracles is not past.
The promises of God are still potent
    still true
  still valid.
He has not lost any of His power, nor has His willingness to help us evaporated.

We are as precious to Him in these days of the twentieth century as were our fathers and their fathers, and the men and women of old who found God a very present help in time of trouble.

Let us not overlook the fact that God often works His miracles in unmiraculous procedures. A baby's tears are not miraculous, yet they were enough to float the ship of God's providence.

We look out on the dreary round and the monotony that eats like acid into our happiness, and wish for wings to fly away from it all and have a change, or pray-dream of some stroke of God's grace whereby in an instant all of life might be changed for us, without our being changed for life.

But not so. God does not work that way.

You long sometimes for some manifestation of God's particular and personal interest in you as an individual. Would you have Him speak your name so that others might hear it, or invest you with some unearthly glow that others could recognize as coming from God? Would you have Him give you powers that would make your life different?

Don't think of it that way. Why, the natural is ever full of the supernatural! The manifestations of God are lying at your feet, cradled in the soil
    they surround you everywhere in the ordinary
    things of everyday
        providence is plucking at your sleeve
        as you walk down the street
God is speaking to you all the time
    in the lines of the book you are reading
        in a letter
            sometimes even in a movie
            or at a concert.
Yes, He speaks to you in music and in your daily duties in the office and in the kitchen.

Did the cherry blossoms say anything to you? Did the azaleas and the wisteria? Had the trees no message for you?
What about this new day? Did it not speak? And the evenings, with their stars?

Have you considered the miracle of the Church? The living Word of God that has survived the efforts of its enemies to destroy it and the indifference of its friends to ignore it? Have you thought of the Lord's Supper, using ordinary bread and grape-juice as the natural wrappings in which comes to you the blessed and gracious ministry of the Holy Spirit?

Have you weighed the miracle of prayer, that you and I together can talk to God and call to the switch-board of our intercession the host of God's angels, the messengers of His mercy and His love that brings into hospital rooms the gracious presence of the Great Physician?

The saving of Moses' life as a little baby, in order that he might grow up to become a liberator, a great statesman, that was all done through the medium of a baby's cry. Behold a miracle in the most natural thing you can think of—the tears of a baby.

God has a hand in our affairs, even from the beginning. This was certainly true of Moses. But it is also true of you and you and of me.
The baby wept at precisely the right moment, otherwise the little cradle might have been overlooked, drifted down-stream or been crushed in the powerful jaws of a crocodile.

Maybe to you the universe looks like a crazy-quilt of haphazard events determined by chance and caprice, with destiny decided by the flip of a coin. But no scientist believes that.

I don't believe it. I firmly believe that God has a plan and purpose for every human life.

That some people never find it, and therefore miss true happiness, is no argument against this conviction of mine, but rather a sad illustration of man's free will to make choices.

The people who make their own decisions are never really happy.

True happiness for any of us lies in our discovering and doing whatever happens to be God's will for our lives. It is only when we are doing our God-appointed function in life that we are really and truly happy.

If we find and obey the plan of God for our lives, there is neither wind nor sea. Neither man nor devil that can defeat us.
If you don't believe that—then your world is a chaos of two billion souls without rhyme or reason, like ships without rudders, living for no purpose, and you are adrift in a world that doesn't make sense.

If there is no Providence, then there is no meaning to life, and it remains a mystery.

But Jesus did not so understand it. Nor did He so teach it.

You say there is no divinity that shapes our ends, rough-hew them how we will.

Well, an Egyptian princess pulls a small water-proof cradle out of the water, and when she pulls aside the blankets, she has pity on a little child, for behold, the baby cried.

And that baby was Moses.

It was the tears of little Moses that saved his life, and it was the God Who was caring for him, Who arranged it that way.

Set in Linotype Aldus, a roman with old-face
characteristics, designed by Hermann Zapf.
Typography by Grant Dahlstrom,
set at The Castle Press.
Printed on Hallmark Eggshell Book paper.
Designed by John F. Hackler.